True Success
Ideas About Living And Loving In An Unbalanced World

James Shelton Wells, Jr., M.D.

CENTER FOR CREATIVE BALANCE

If your bookstore does not have *True Success*, copies can be obtained by writing or calling:

Center for Creative Balance
P.O. Box 16562
Chapel Hill, North Carolina 27514
(919) 967-6353

Cover Art from a pastel drawing entitled "Snowed in With Thoughts of Spring" by Carolyn Aaronson, Durham, NC. Courtesy of Susan Reintjes.

Design and Production by Martha Lorantos, Chapel Hill, NC
Editing by Patricia Davis and Libba Wells
Printed at Ferguson Printing, Durham, NC

To my wife, Libba;
my children, Peter and Mark;
my parents and brothers;
and to all who seek
peace and harmony
in themselves, their families
and throughout the world.

Preface

This book has been partially excerpted from a previous publication by the author entitled *A Psychology of Love.* Both books encourage the day-to-day practice of principles which can help us secure our daily supply of life's necessities and secure that supply in ways which are more loving for ourselves and equally for others. It is not the intention of the author to advocate any particular religious or political creed.

It is hoped that you will contemplate each page and focus on evaluating its relevance for you personally. If a particular page has special meaning for you, you may wish to open the book to that page and leave it in a conspicuous place. Please also feel free to duplicate a page and put it up somewhere as a frequent reminder to you of a particular helpful idea.

It is also recommended that if you have found the material helpful, systematically re-read it on a regular basis. The author, in fact, reads several pages daily in order to reinforce the principles which he has found to be helpful. Meditation following reading opens our spirits to more fully learn what we need to about loving ourselves and others and getting what we need in positive ways.

That which is true in these pages is believed to be a gift from a Power greater than the author, as well as from the author's many teachers who are fellow travellers through this life.

*True success
is being able to obtain
our day-to-day basic needs
while maintaining a loving attitude
toward ourselves and others.*

This implies that in our day-to-day living, we will attempt to balance work, recreation, contemplation, and sharing time with others.

It is desirable for all of these aspects of our lives to reflect a loving attitude toward ourselves and others to the extent of our current ability. Among other things this would mean that we do our work in a way which is satisfying to us and helpful to others. It also means that obtaining more than we need does not make us more successful.

By this definition, we can all achieve success. The severely handicapped may need extra help from others, but even so, we all can feel competent and loving within the framework of our own particular gifts.

Emotional turmoil
(and much physical illness as well)
is usually a manifestation of
our fear that we will not be able
to get all of what we need.
We are often driven to conform
to the prevailing values of our society
(even when this is not really
in our best interests)
in hopes that we can be more secure.

◆〉══◉══〈◆

There are, of course, biological factors which may be sufficient to cause illness or contribute to illness. Even in those instances, however, if we feel insecure or inadequate, these feelings can be made worse by our inability to be what our society values most. And this is likely to intensify an emotional or physical problem or provide a major obstacle to its resolution.

Our western society
values and rewards people who are:

MALE
(the more "masculine" the better — if female, then the more pleasing to males the better)

HETEROSEXUAL
(happily married with "successful" children)

WHITE
(often in the USA and UK also must be Anglo-Saxon and Protestant)

YOUNG
(and healthy without handicaps)

BEAUTIFUL
(tall, thin, and well-dressed)

WELL-EDUCATED
(at the most prestigious institutions and have an appearance of sophistication)

WEALTHY
(with impressive house, cars, boats, vacation home, luxurious dining, impressive club memberships – to name a few of the often sought signs of wealth)

POWERFUL
(prestigious position)

EMOTIONALLY PERFECT
(without anger [unless righteous indignation], without tears, without depression, without anxiety, and without negative thoughts)

Success in our western culture is believed by most of us to be determined by the extent to which we fulfill these characteristics or at least appear to fulfill them.

The frantic pursuit of these social values or characteristics is maintained by a fear that without these characteristics we cannot secure our supply of life's necessities. We also fear ridicule or more subtle rejection from parents, authority figures, and peers if we are not these things.

We as a culture have come to value maleness because males have been physically stronger on average than females and could defend us against attack from other men or wild animals. We value power because we believe that if we have it, we will be safe from everything but death from old age. We believe that if we are all the things listed above we will be able to provide for all our needs including being safe from intimidation, humiliation, and embarassment. If we are sufficiently powerful, we believe no one can rob us of our home, food, clothes, or toys. We believe no other men will steal a powerful man's possessions or women (which men have traditionally considered possessions).

The fear of losing what we need has set up a vicious cycle of feelings of powerlessness, prompting efforts to gain power. We will try to gain power directly or through any means available to us. Sometimes we may even act weak in order to gain power over an intimidating person who needs to feel strong. We may use sex to gain power, or we may dominate those weaker than we are. Those who are weaker than we are are fearful too and try to gain power in the same ways over those who are weaker still. Unfortunately, this is often a child who grows up afraid and tends to repeat the cycle in one way or another.

Fearful men tend to dominate women, other men, and children. Fearful women dominate children and less powerful women and men. The cycle only ends when love, sharing, cooperation, enlightment, and forgiveness replace fear.

True success is not achieved by being male, heterosexual, white, young, beautiful, well-educated, wealthy, powerful, and emotionally perfect but rather by being able to obtain our daily basic needs while being loving toward ourselves and each other.

Pretense is an effort
to avoid embarassment
or humiliation over not being
what we think is expected of
a "successful" person.

-<>=●=<>-

In other words, if we aren't what we think we should be, then there is a tendency to *pretend* to be what we think we should be.

William James didn't see much value in pretense and suggested the following equation:

$$\text{SELF-ESTEEM} = \frac{\text{SUCCESS (actual accomplishments)}}{\text{PRETENSE (unfulfilled expectations which we are pretending to have accomplished)}}$$

Obviously, in this equation as pretense goes up, self-esteem goes down!

When thinking of being loving toward ourselves,

Love is patient and kind.
I am patient with myself;
I do my best for myself;
I do not resent myself;

Love is not ill-mannered or irritable.
I do not belittle myself;
I do not have unrealistic expectations of myself;
I am not discourteous to myself;
I do not get irritated with myself;

Love is not jealous, conceited, or proud.
I do not isolate myself from others;

Love does not keep a record of wrongs.
I do not identify myself with my bad points;
I am never condemning of myself;

Love does not like evil (hurtful, excluding behavior)
I am not grimly satisfied with myself when I do wrong...

But is happy with the truth.
...on the contrary, I am pleased when I do right;

Love never gives up, and its faith, hope and patience never fail.
I am always loyal to myself;
I am always hopeful for myself;
I always bear with myself.

Adapted from Today's English Version of Paul's First Letter to the Corinthians, Chapter 13, verses 4-7 and from a personal letter from Roger J. Corless dated December 17, 1986.

THE GOLDEN RULE:

*Do unto others
as we would have them do unto us,
is essential, and so is its corollary:
Do unto ourselves
as we would do unto others.*

If we would not be rude, disrespectful, unkind, or irritable to others, then why should we be rude, disrespectful, unkind, or irritable to ourselves?

A positive restatement of both the Golden Rule and its corollary might be:

*Be loving toward others as we would have others be
loving toward us, while being just as loving toward
ourselves as we are toward others.*

*We are so sensitive to criticism
and often are excessively critical
of ourselves because
from birth we began
to scan the world around us
and were especially sensitive
to the facial expressions and
voice inflections
of our parents and other caregivers
for signs of approval and disapproval.*

Because children respond to parents and caregivers in this way, learning occurs about what is safe or dangerous, what is acceptable or unacceptable, what is appropriate or inappropriate, and what is helpful and unhelpful.

Caregivers (parents or otherwise) will contribute through these interactions toward shaping our behavior and value system. If the predominant response to us is DELIGHT, and the predominant attitudes of our caregivers are characterized by patience, kindness, and tolerant acceptance of our attempts to learn helpful from hurtful behaviors, we are likely to feel valued and acceptable even if our behavior falls short of that desired by the caregivers. Clear limits on (and clear explanations of) potentially hurtful behavior with age-appropriate and behavior-appropriate consequences, which are consistently applied when the limits are exceeded, are also helpful to our learning while maintaining our sense of acceptance as a person. In other words, we can keep our acceptance as a person separate from approval or disapproval of our behavior or performance.

If, on the other hand, the caregivers have equated their own worth or sense of acceptability with adherence to prevailing cultural standards of acceptability, then the caregiver will tend to exhibit a lack of tolerance, patience, and kindness toward us and themselves when the standards aren't met. This is likely to result in a tendency by us to equate the parental disapproval of our behavior with disapproval of us. Our sense of self-worth will be diminished, and we are likely to either strive intensely to attain the prevailing standards or rebel against one or more of them. In either case, however, we will measure ourselves against these standards in one way or another.

It is desirable to respect our parents as people in a position of responsibility who probably have done and are doing the best they can given the circumstances of their own lives. It is important, on the other hand, not to embrace any of their values which do not reflect a loving attitude toward themselves and others (especially toward their child). This means it is helpful to reject any hurtful behavior by our parents while trying to the best of our ability to accept them as people who have acted hurtfully out of their own immaturity, fear, or ignorance.

*Being patient with ourselves
and avoiding
condemnation of ourselves
are especially important
and very difficult,*

particularly for any of us who have not
been treated patiently and kindly or who
have experienced frequent negative
(condemning) criticism. This criticism
may have been either verbal or non-
verbal through body language. Abusive
behavior of any kind by a parent toward
a child is always experienced as
degrading and condemning.

*We can know we are lovable
when we have once seen it
reflected in the face of another.*

If no one has ever delighted in us for
simply being, it is difficult, if not
impossible, for us to know that we are
lovable. We may believe we are
appreciated for what we do, yet we may
still feel empty and unlovable.

If we frequently experienced parental
distress and never had anyone who
delighted in us for simply being, we may
even think: "If there is a God, and God
loves some people, then for some reason
God must not love me."

When we don't feel lovable,
we often work real hard
looking for love, and often
"in all the wrong places."

Modern-day Pharisees look for love in a wrong place.

Those of us who are into strict adherence to some kind of religious doctrine seem to be trying to find acceptance through the competitive devotion to the rules of religion.

Yuppies may look for love in a wrong place.

We seem to be trying to find acceptance through prestigious jobs, homes, cars, club memberships, graduation from prestigious colleges, having our children take music, horseback riding, dance, tennis, and more.

Do-gooders may look for love in a wrong place.

We seem to be trying to find acceptance through ostentatious (or this may be contrived humility instead) and often frenetically pursued good works like participation in a shelter for the homeless, Meals on Wheels, outreach to prisons, and more.

Academicians may look for love in a wrong place.

We often seem to be trying to find acceptance through a display of our industriousness and our knowledge by acquiring degrees and writing papers and books for a vitae and acclaim.

Fastidious housekeepers may look for love in a wrong place.

We often seem to be trying to find acceptance through extreme attention to maintaining cleanliness.

Health enthusiasts may look for love in a wrong place.

We often seem to be trying to find acceptance through our adherence to what we believe to be the rules of fitness; for example, exercise, meditation, weight control, vegetarian diet, and more.

All of the activities mentioned above may have beneficial personal and social effects and are not undesirable in and of themselves. They will not alone, however, provide us with a sense of being acceptable no matter how vigorously we pursue them.

What we in these categories haven't discovered is that we can be lovable — we can be acceptable — without the <u>excessive</u> pursuit of these activities. Being more relaxed about what we do can still allow for an experience of agency in the world without diminishing our acceptance. This will also allow us to enjoy more of what we do.

In our quest to gain love or acceptance through frenetic activities, all of us in these and similar categories can inadvertently contribute to our own suffering and to that of others in our various communities.

Joy is a gift worth celebrating and enhancing wherever, whenever, and to whatever extent possible.

It is important to look for joy in everyday experiences. Hurry and lack of patience make it difficult if not impossible to see the joyful aspects of our everyday lives.

According to Henry David Thoreau, "We have lived not in proportion to the number of years we have spent on the earth but in proportion as we have enjoyed."

Happiness and inner peace come from:

Solving problems creatively.

Solving problems in cooperation with other people.

Appreciating with all our senses the beauty of the world around us.

Doing our chosen work skillfully and faithfully.

Listening to God's spirit which affirms that our life matters and that we are loved by God.

Asking forgiveness of and making amends to those whom we have hurt if doing so will not hurt them more.

Accepting that there are some situations we cannot change — at least for now.

Helping others.

Living within our time and energy means.

Spending time with friends whom we appreciate and who appreciate us.

Living within our monetary means.

Taking care of ourselves physically through a balanced diet and regular exercise.

Touching lovingly and being touched lovingly by someone who shares in our life and accepts us as we are.

Some loving ways in which we can shift toward taking better care of ourselves and thereby be more prepared to experience joy and happiness include:

sensible eating, regular exercise
(with stretching
before and after),
meditation, study and
contemplation, adequate rest,
and in general seeking moderation
(avoiding extremes).

It is very important, however, to avoid condemnation of ourselves for not doing the above or only partially doing so.

*Being truly loving
toward ourselves
actually makes it easier
to share love with others.*

Sharing means giving of our resources to someone else in need.

This can have real value for the recipient(s) and the giver. It feels good to share.

It is important, however, not to deplete ourselves to such an extent that our own needs are not being met. This leads to burnout. Balance is the key. It is important to remember that no one person is the sole repository of goodness in the world.

Sometimes giving to someone who doesn't really need our help can foster excessive dependency on us, which is not helpful and may even be harmful. It can inadvertently rob someone of an opportunity to experience their own ability to solve problems. Giving just enough help and not too much is the optimal way to share.

Freely given service to others is usually not so much self-sacrifice but, rather, self-renewal through sharing.

We have probably all heard it said that we gain our lives by losing them. What does this mean? Well, whatever else it may mean, it suggests that we receive a sense of renewal and purpose if we give up our self-centered brooding about what isn't the way we would like it to be and focus at least part of our time on voluntarily serving the needs of others without any expectation of payback of any sort from anybody.

There may be times when one of us will make a self-sacrifice of some kind in order that another of us can receive something especially needed.

There are some situations in which the sacrifice of a few (from giving up dinner or sleep or some other relative need or comfort to the voluntary risk of or even loss of life) is desirable. This may be a loving and needed way for one person to respond to another. A parent, for example, may give up sleep to attend a sick child. Those individuals who worked to contain the nuclear reactor disaster at Chernobyl are an extreme example of necessary and desirable voluntary self-sacrifice.

It is not helpful to us, however, when we have been self-sacrificial in some way to think that we are more or less worthwhile than the person or persons for whom we have made the sacrifice. We have simply been able for various reasons to provide something which was needed at a time when it was needed.

If we are a "martyr", we tend to derive our sense of self-worth through a pattern of excessive voluntary self-sacrifice. If we are a "scapegoat", we may also eventually come to derive self-worth from self-sacrifice, though initially at least it was imposed upon us by others.

The only truly satisfying relationships are those in which we convey and perceive mutual respect and value without one of us being self-sacrificial any more often than the other (unless one of us has an excess supply of something really needed by another, and this would be more like sharing than self-sacrifice).

When thinking of being loving toward others,

Love is slow to lose patience.

May I be content to wait without becoming angry when others fall below the expectations I have set for them.

Love is kind and constructive.

May I be cautious in my judgments towards others and honestly seek to be a healing rather than a hurting presence in my relationships.

Love is not possessive.

May I not have to be in control of every conversation and situation.

Love is not anxious to impress.

May I relax with whomever I am associated and not feel I have to be the life of the party in order to feel secure.

Love is not arrogant.

May I have a balanced view of my place in the body of humankind.

Love has good manners.

May I respect the rights and dignity of others enough not to force thoughtless behavior upon them.

Love is not self-centered.

May I find pleasure in the happiness of others.

(Adapted from a responsive reading which was part of a worship service at The Olin T. Binkley Memorial Baptist Church, Chapel Hill, NC, in March 1984.)

Women and men in general and men and women as individuals have differences and equal value.

If our telephone requires repair, then a neurosurgeon who doesn't know about repairing telephones is not likely to be very helpful.

If our shirt needs mending, then a lawyer who doesn't know how to sew is not likely to be very helpful.

If our water pipe bursts, then a professor who doesn't know about plumbing is not likely to be very helpful.

If our child needs teaching, then an astronaut who doesn't relate well to children is not likely to be very helpful.

And so it goes. We all need one another. Sometimes we may need a certain person and their attributes more than anyone else, yet on balance, women and men in general and men and women as individuals have differences and equal value.

Patience
(with ourselves and each other)
is probably the most
important characteristic of love.

Patience does not mean avoiding all confrontation, but it does mean letting go of (not sweating) the small stuff. It does mean avoiding personal attacks and condemning intonations and expressions when confronting what we believe to be undesirable attitudes and behaviors in each other (including our children and our mates) or ourselves.

It is helpful when attempting to be patient with others to think about how we would feel if our situations were reversed.

Sharing information about our preferences and opinions can be very helpful in our relationships with each other, while reprimands, admonitions, and condescending attitudes are less likely to be helpful and may even be very hurtful and harmful (the more severe and more frequent, the more hurtful and harmful). When we have acted in these negative ways, an apology is almost always in order and can help temper the damage we have done.

It is important to remember that we get angry and lose patience out of fear that we are going to lose something we need. If we can identify the fear, we often can regain our patience as we consider whether what we need is really currently threatened or whether there is some other way to obtain what we need.

Anger is
a normal human emotion
filled with energy.

-+>==0==+>

Having a loving attitude does not preclude being angry sometimes.

Anger is always a response to frustration and fear. Because of its energy, it can be an important component in changing attitudes and behaviors which are unhelpful, or it can be an unhelpful, destructive force which compounds our frustration, fear, or sadness. It is what we do with our angry feelings which makes all the difference. It is always important to transform our energy which is coming from anger into positive rather than negative action.

It is sometimes helpful to transform our anger by vigorous physical exercise. This can clear our minds and allow us to consider our options without the confusion of severe anger. After vigorous exercise, writing down our angry feelings rather than exploding them verbally can often be a constructive way to express anger and perhaps understand its source. After writing down our feelings, we may want to share what we have written with the person with whom we are angry and ask them to respond to us in writing. This will often help diffuse the intensity of the anger and lead to a solution.

When we're irritable or
otherwise feeling angry,
it is because we are feeling threatened.
It can be helpful to ask ourselves
"from where does my fear and anger
really come? Is my life really in
immediate danger?"

Anger always has beneath it frustration and fear.

This frustration and fear often have more to do with previous situations or with other people we have known than with our present circumstances.

Very intensely felt emotions usually are drawing their extreme intensity from past experiences. We may fear (conscious or otherwise) that previous insecurities, hurts, or threats will be experienced again in the present or future.

Professions of love
are truly meaningful
only when accompanied
by loving behavior.

If we tell other people that we love them, yet talk to them in a condemning, condescending, or perpetually dissatisfied manner, then our professions of love are not likely to be heard as sincere expressions of our true feelings. If we say we love others and then put them down or fail to consider their point of view with respect, then we are very likely to convey ill-mannered, aggressive, or passive-aggressive hostility rather than love.

If we say we love others and then ignore their real needs for food, clothing, shelter, safety, nurture, and acceptance, which we have the means to provide, then we will convey at the very least indifference rather than love.

If we say to ourselves that we intend to act in more loving ways toward ourselves and then persistently put ourselves down, overextend our resources, or avoid changing our unhelpful and harmful attitudes and behaviors, which we are capable of changing, then we are not likely to believe our professions of love for ourselves.

It has been said that "talk is cheap." Our professions of love must be accompanied by loving actions in order for them to reach full or complete fruition.

Sincere expressions of gratitude are very important in loving relationships.

When someone we love does something we appreciate, it is very important to let them know of our appreciation. Saying "thank you" only takes an instant, yet its impact is enduring.

"Thank you" gives positive re-enforcement to our children when their behavior is on target, and "thank you" lets our adult partners, friends and co-workers know they are not taken for granted. "Thank you" acknowledges the help of strangers, and "thank you" lifts the spirits of longtime servants who faithfully perform their duties. These servants include our barbers, nurses, fathers, secretaries, physicians, waitpersons, tailors, clergypersons, cooks, housekeepers, lawyers, mothers, baby sitters, dentists, teachers, storeclerks, and others.

Being loving toward others
includes being kind and being helpful
and does not include
trying to think for others
when they can think
quite well for themselves
or doing for others
when they can do
quite well for themselves.

Pitching in to help with a task is very different from taking over responsibility for the task.

Offering suggestions when they are requested is very different from giving unsolicited or unnecessary advice.

It is also helpful to remember that asking for or giving suggestions does not mean the suggestions have to be followed. Our value as a person does not depend upon having our suggestions followed.

We have responsibilities _to_ others and few responsibilities _for_ others.

We may have responsibilities <u>to</u> others for certain behaviors, either by convention or because we have willingly accepted these responsibilities. However, we have very few responsibilities <u>for</u> the behavior of others. We may influence but are not responsible for the thoughts and feelings of others. All of us are responsible for our own thoughts and feelings, and all adults are responsible for their own behavior. Adults have to be responsible for the behavior of very young children. As children grow older, they are able to assume more and more responsibility for themselves, and it is helpful for adults to relinquish all age-appropriate responsibilities to the child.

Discipline
when appropriately applied
is loving.
Being loving toward ourselves and others does not imply being permissive toward ourselves or others when what is needed is kind, consistent, and firm limit setting.

Limits are needed whenever a behavior is likely to be hurtful in some way to ourselves or to others.

Rules and consequences are designed to help avoid hurtful behavior and are a form of limit setting. Rules and consequences which have already been discussed require very little, if any, further discussion at the time the rules are broken. It is then time for consequences not discussion. Further discussion about feelings related to the rules, and their consequences when broken, is always appropriate but only after indicated disciplinary actions have been taken.

Discipline does not mean inflicting physical or emotional injury.

The old maxim "spare the rod and spoil the child" has been widely misinterpreted. Would shepherds beat their sheep when they go astray? Certainly not! If for no other reason, they would not want to damage their valuable property. While our children are not our property, most of us don't want to damage them. If we damage them, it is generally done inadvertently by following the examples of our parents who were following the examples of their parents. Most of the examples passed on to us by our parents are very beneficial, yet some of them cause us real pain and cause us to inflict real pain on our children. The inappropriate use of a "rod" is one way we can unintentionally harm our children by following the examples of our parents.

A rod does not have to be used for inflicting or threatening injury. It can be used as a prod to gently encourage a sheep or a child in the right direction. This kind of rod may take the form of a non-injurious single spank to the bottom or the hands of a toddler, or it may mean losing the privilege of using a car for a time for a teenager.

Trying to humiliate children in order to get them to behave differently is never appropriate, for humiliation causes injury to the spirit. This always makes a problem worse rather than better.

Constructive criticism begins with "I".

We are able to hear the helpful, critical comments of others if they preface their remarks with "I statements." In other words, we are much more likely to listen to someone else's opinion when it is stated as their opinion rather than as definitive, objective truth as perceived by every reasonable person everywhere.

When we, ourselves, are offering our opinions to others, we are more likely to be heard in a positive way if we begin our statements with phrases like, "I may be wrong about this, yet this is the way I see..." or "My opinion of...is..." or "I'm feeling...and would like to share my thoughts with you. Would you be willing to listen to what I have to say?" or "I would really like for you to hear my opinion about...May I share it with you?"

It is further likely to be helpful if we conclude our critical remarks with sincere expressions of appreciation for something we believe the other person is doing or has done "right."

Unsolicited criticism usually does little to change our immature thoughts and actions.

If we ask for the opinions of others about our ideas or behaviors, then their constructive criticism can be very useful to us.

Similarly, if others ask us if we would like their opinions about something we have said or done or anticipate saying or doing, and we say we would like to hear their opinion, then their constructive comments can again be very helpful.

Criticism, on the other hand, which is offered without having been requested or without our having acceded to hearing it, is more difficult to accept. It can still be helpful, especially if it is constructive, but we are less likely to be open to hearing it with a positive attitude.

Unsolicited, negative, or derogatory criticism only tends to contribute to a hardening of our attitudes and behaviors even if we are thinking or doing something which is unhelpful or harmful and would have benefited from what was being said.

Children often need the benefit of adult experience and more mature understanding to help them positively shape their attitudes and behaviors. However, we adults have to remember that children also will be less open to hearing negative, derogatory criticism than they would be to hearing constructive comments which are offered at their request or with their permission.

Even with young children we can say, "Will you let me show you how I do that?" or "Will you let me explain how I think about that?" or "I'd like to tell you what I expect of you in this situation, would you please listen to what I have to say?"

While there may be times when we just have to correct a child without any preamble of this kind, we will get further with children, and adults also for that matter, if we use this approach as often as possible. By doing this we are not giving in to another's inappropriate behavior, but rather showing our respect for their autonomy and a desire for them to show us similar respect.

If nothing a child (or an adult who is close to us) does is ever quite good enough for us, and we find ourselves constantly on their backs with negative criticism, then we will probably contribute more to their frustration than to their ability to alter inappropriate behavior.

Sarcasm and passive aggression are defenses which are dangerous for all concerned.

Initially motivated by fear of domination or humiliation, sarcasm and passive aggression easily become habits which are hard to break. These interpersonal behavior patterns may develop in response to teenage peer teasing, parental modeling, or parental overcontrol and excessive negative criticism. Whatever the cause of the initial sarcastic or passive aggressive behaviors, their habitual use causes emotional pain and often induces similar responses from others in retaliation.

"I was just teasing," or "Can't you take a joke?" are frequent rejoinders when sarcastic remarks are confronted, yet the "teasing" or "joking" has already had its painful, sharply cutting effects.

Passive aggression is often disguised as efforts to be helpful to someone while actually being motivated by a desire to put them down. "Killing someone with kindness" is in this category. There's always the potential for deniability when confronted, yet as with sarcasm, the damage has been done.

If we have become habitually sarcastic or passively aggressive, it is helpful to remind ourselves of the likely negative consequences and find alternative, more direct ways to express our feelings of dissatisfaction and anger. Constructive "I statements" are probably most appropriate in most situations.

It's not just what we say that's important, but also how and when we say it.

While our words may convey one message, our intonations, facial expressions, mannerisms, and timing may convey quite a different message.

If people around us don't seem to respond to what seems to us to be our reasonable statements, then it may be because of how or when we said what we did.

Sometimes we can express love and patience with words while actually conveying indifference, hostility, or impatience through our voice inflections, the glare in our eyes, and the tension in our body. By like token, some of us with a rough exterior who profess indifference may express with our actions real tenderness and concern.

If there is no good reason
to say "no" to a child
(or an adult for that matter),
then say "yes."
If there is a good reason to say "no,"
then say "no"
clearly, kindly, and firmly.

Children and others need to know that there are limits – that instant gratification of our wants and even our needs is not always going to be possible or even desirable. We as individuals, and in communities with others, will not benefit from the excesses of action or inaction to which we might be inclined due to either biological or learned influences.

Good reasons for saying "no" include situations in which the behavior is likely to be hurtful directly or indirectly through the inappropriate use of scarce resources.

*It is better
to say "no" right away
than to make promises
we know now we cannot keep.*

It is better to say "maybe" if the circumstances are *really* not yet clear, and we
would like to say "yes" given the right
circumstances which could possibly still
develop.

Before making a decision
which will affect other people,
it is usually helpful
to discuss the pros and cons
with the people involved.

Whenever possible, this also applies to decisions which will affect children.

Whenever considering any behavior which will possibly affect another person of any age, it is helpful to ask ourselves how we would feel about the behavior if we were the other person.

We are all human. It is important to be forgiving of ourselves (not condemning of ourselves) for those times when we have had unloving attitudes and for those times when we have shown unloving behavior toward ourselves or others.

Evaluating ourselves for unloving attitudes and unhelpful or hurtful behavior toward ourselves or others is desirable. It will help us have more loving attitudes and behavior in the present or future when faced with the same or similar situations.

It is not desirable, however, to be condemning of ourselves for anything.

We all have impatient, unkind, possessive, ill-mannered, self-centered, jealous, greedy, and arrogant impulses as part of both our biological and learned natures.

There is no benefit in trying to deny that we have these impulses. They are a part of us, and it is unhelpful for us to condemn these impulses.

We do need to control our unloving behaviors to the best of our ability, but we also need to be accepting of ourselves even with our unloving impulses.

*We sometimes tend
to project onto others
what we we most object to
in ourselves.*

In other words, we often complain loudest about someone else's behavior (especially someone close to us) when it is behavior we have trouble controlling in ourselves. We may even accuse others of things they have not done in an unconscious attempt to deny that very kind of behavior or associated attitudes in ourselves. It is important to look at ourselves before blaming someone else for what we believe has gone wrong in our lives.

We may also project onto others threatening characteristics of our early caregivers over whom we had little if any control. We do this in an effort to repeat the earlier trauma, this time hoping to gain mastery over the previously overwhelming experience.

All of us
have behaved
in hurtful ways
because of our immaturity.

When we realize that we have acted in
immature, unhelpful, or hurtful ways, it is
important to forgive ourselves for this
kind of childish behavior and live as
maturely as possible in the present.

A Checklist for Evaluating Our Maturity

These are some of the more important characteristics of a mature adult:

1. *We do not automatically resent criticism because we realize that it may contain a suggestion for improving ourselves.*

2. *We know that self-pity is futile and childish — a way of placing the blame for our disappointments on others.*

3. *We do not lose our temper readily or allow ourselves to "fly off the handle" about trifles.*

4. *We keep our head in emergencies and deal with them in a logical, reasonable fashion.*

5. *We accept responsibility for our acts and decisions and do not blame someone else when things go wrong.*

6. *We accept reasonable delays without impatience, realizing that we must adjust ourselves to the convenience of others on some occasions.*

7. We are a good loser, accepting defeat and disappointment without complaint or ill temper.

8. We do not worry unduly about things we can't do anything about.

9. We don't boast or "show off," but when we are praised or complimented, we accept the praise with grace and appreciation and without false modesty.

10. We applaud others' achievements with sincere good will.

11. We rejoice in the good fortune and success of others because we have outgrown petty jealousy and envy.

12. We listen courteously to the opinions of others and, even when they hold opposing views, do not enter into hostile argument.

13. We do not find fault with "every little thing" or criticize people who do things of which we might not approve unless the issues of concern are likely to be seriously harmful to that person or to others (and then we find the most helpful way possible to convey our concerns).

14. *We make reasonable plans for our activities and try to carry them out in an orderly fashion; we do not do things too quickly without due consideration of the consequences. We are, at the same time, able to be spontaneous and flexible when unexpected opportunities arise or circumstances indicate a need for a change in our plans.*

15. *We show spiritual maturity by:*

accepting the fact that a Power greater than ourselves has an important place in our lives.

realizing we are part of humankind as a whole, that our fellows have much to give us, and that we have an obligation to share with others the gifts that we have received.

obeying the spirit of the Golden Rule: "Do unto others as we would have them do unto us."

Adapted from Moral and Spiritual Values used by the Los Angeles, California, city schools in their education program. I first saw it in the AL-ANON booklet <u>Alcoholism is a Family Disease.</u>

*It is important to remember
we are all uniquely special
without being the best or better
than anyone else.*

Competition is probably the result of both biological and socially shaped (learned) influences.

Competition has probably had some usefulness to our society, especially in the history of humanity when survival of the fittest probably played an important role in the survival of the human species.

At this point in our world, however, the survival of the species is not likely to depend upon competition but rather upon cooperation.

Competition can promote industriousness, which gets socially desirable projects accomplished. All too often, however, we carry it too far and begin jockeying for positions in the social pecking order, which is based upon misplaced values. This is not likely to foster a cooperative spirit but rather jealousy, arrogant pride, and unhelpful conflict.

There is a natural tendency for every child to not only want to feel appreciated and affirmed but also to want to be more appreciated and more special than everyone else (especially more than brothers and sisters). This wish may drive us to incredible competition with one another, always with ever increasing stakes. The only relief from this "rat race" is to discover that we all have a unique specialness which does not depend upon being the best or better than anyone else.

Competitive team sports in our society probably perpetuate to some significant degree sexist and jockeying-for-position attitudes. On the other hand, sports allow for mastery experiences — opportunities to develop competence and confidence. They also have the redeeming qualities of encouraging at least small group cooperation and playing by fair rules, which in some sports discourage physical injury. To the extent advocated, the attitude that how one plays is more important than winning or losing is also valuable, as is, of course, the physical exercise and the healthy release of our aggressive feelings.

Why do we have trouble loving others?

All of us have the same basic needs for food (an adequate amount), clothing, shelter, safety (from physical or emotional dangers including safety from violence toward us from others and from having our emotional boundaries violated), nurture (caring touch, encouraging words, and other expressions of love), and acceptance (affirmation of our value to others in our community–from family to increasingly larger communities of which we are a part).

Since we want to be sure we have enough of what we need, we all want to <u>control</u> our supply of these basic necessities of life. When this desire for control becomes excessive, it blocks our ability to love.

Anyone who we perceive as a threat to our supply of life's necessities becomes our rival. This may as easily be a sister or brother, spouse or friend as someone we would identify as an enemy.

All excesses in our behavior
are ways in which we are
trying to cope with our fears
that we will not get our needs met.

We overeat in search of nurture and acceptance.

Overeating may be a way of searching for nurture or coping with our frustrations over feeling inadequate in our quest for acceptance.

If we are feeling lonely or unloved, we may turn to food in an attempt to satisfy our longings and frustrations. Food, of course, can do this only to the extent that it has been associated with an earlier caregiver who perhaps cuddled us and cooed at us. If there isn't this association, eating is simply an instinct which demands satiation and has been substituted for our unsatisfied longings for nurture and acceptance. We can momentarily feel comforted because we are at least getting plenty of one of our basic needs, the need for food.

Overeating can also occur when we are tired and in need of rest but are unwilling or unable to stop our activities long enough to get the rest we need. Our fatigue might also be helped by invigorating exercise, yet we are unwilling or unable to use this energizing approach either. Food, in this case, can become a hoped for solution to our lack of energy. The problem, of course, is that this solution is temporary at best.

When overeating leads to being overweight, we tend to put ourselves down because we do not conform to a particular body image on which society has placed value, no matter how misplaced this value may be. Some of us will further use this lack of conformity to confirm the negative messages others have given us. Others of us will use being overweight to avoid intimacy which has become threatening to us for various reasons, often because our personal boundaries have been violated.

Still others of us will overeat in binges and then purge ourselves of what we have eaten by vomiting or using laxatives. While this behavior may have a range of symbolic significance for us, it is at least another way to attempt to gain control of some element of our lives over which we feel we have no control.

In our consumer-oriented society, shopping can be a way of soothing our hurts and seeking approval from others (those we know and those who write the advertisements).

We are constantly barraged by catchy TV commercials which employ sexual innuendos, "beautiful" and "successful" people, and popular tunes changed to plug a product. We are told both directly and more subtly that if we possess these products, we will impress our friends, enjoy a position of importance, and generally demonstrate our intelligence and good taste. If these attributes we are supposed to gain seem somewhat redundant, so are the commercials.

As a result of our frequent exposure to this kind of coercion, almost all of us have complied to some extent through compulsive buying. We buy the latest fashions, the most convenient appliances and other gadgets, the most prestigious automobiles, the most exciting recreation equipment and accessories, and the longest lasting, most success-inducing deodorants. We buy and buy and buy.

Some of us are especially prone to buy when we are feeling lonely, bored, sad, or unlovable. We seem to think that the commercials are true—that we will be more popular, more intelligent, and more successful if we have "the right stuff."

While we may find a number of products convenient, aesthetically pleasing, and fun, we need to think carefully about how we use our (and our world's) supply of scarce resources. We also need to be honest with ourselves about the fact that "the right stuff" alone will not do for us what has been promised.

A gambler is seeking the illusion of control which comes when we are winning against the odds.

We may even feel a magical sense of specialness when we are winning — a sense that "the gods must be with us" or "lady luck is smiling at us." Some of us may even say when we are in a winning streak, "I must be living right."

The problem, of course, is that we don't always win and are as likely to have losing streaks as winning streaks. Neither winning nor losing have very much if anything to do with our competence, though it is the illusion of competence which we are seeking.

Another problem with gambling when it has become a compulsion is that our judgment concerning the use of our resources has usually become distorted. We put up money we and our communities don't have to lose. Then when we do lose, we may either continue to bet what we cannot afford to lose, go into debt, or feel angry or depressed. If we win, we are very likely to be winning money that someone else cannot afford to lose. This may result in suffering about which we may not ever know, but to which we have contributed.

In short, gambling is not a very balanced or loving way to achieve a sense of personal competence.

*Drug abuse is a way of
chemically inducing
an altered state of consciousness
which temporarily provides either
an illusion of peace and control
or deadening of our feelings of fear
and anxiety which stem from
deprivation of life's necessities,
especially nurture and acceptance.*

The key word above is TEMPORARILY. While some prescribed medicines can contribute toward the alleviation of biologically induced emotional distress for even extended periods of time, commonly abused substances such as alcohol, heroin, tobacco, cocaine, marijuana, and excessive amounts of certain prescription medicines usually provide their effects for limited periods of time and require perpetual use of ever increasing amounts of the substance.

The ultimate outcome of our abuse of these substances is our further alienation from potential sources of the nurture and acceptance for which we long. We leave a trail of unmet responsibilities and directly harmful behavior toward ourselves and others which serves to confirm our already low opinion of ourselves.

To avoid these further feelings of alienation from ourselves, we tend to return to the substance or substances rather than admit our helplessness over our addictions and our need to turn to a Twelve Step Program which will guide us toward our goals of nurture, acceptance, and peace.

There are some among us who have a genetically inherited predisposition for being especially sensitive to decreased supplies of nurture and acceptance. This predisposition also seems to coincide with craving for alcohol and similar substances. The right medications or combinations of medications can sometimes diminish both the craving for alcohol and the extreme sensitivity to feelings of loneliness and rejection. It is still true, however, that the Twelve Step Programs are our best hope for attaining permanently, one day at a time, the relief from our distress which all of us in this group are seeking.

*Workabolism
is an attempt
to achieve mastery
over earlier,
overwhelming
life circumstances.*

Having had an alcoholic, chronically ill, severely depressed, or otherwise impaired parent predisposes us to behavior which we believe will help us avoid feeling as out of control and utterly overwhelmed as we did when we were a child. Overwork can give us the illusion of controlling our chaotic past. When we have taken on so much to do that we are just on the edge of disaster, yet we are still juggling it all through our organized overwork, we are likely to feel the exhilaration of accomplishment and perceived control. When, on the other hand, we become overwhelmed by all we have taken on to do — when we feel like we are going over the edge of disaster, we are likely to feel the same panic we felt in those earlier chaotic experiences of our life. In response, we'll often try to work that much harder. As a result, we tend to develop the proverbial "vicious cycle."

Another reason for over-working includes having received our most positive feedback from our parents or others for this behavior (possibly labeled industriousness). It has become, therefore, a source of affirmation (a necessity of life) which we seek to preserve through the perpetuation of overworking.

The major problem with overworking as a coping strategy is that it frequently doesn't help us avoid the feelings of being overwhelmed, and persistent overworking is dangerous to our health. Working hard is not the same as overworking. "Overwork-ing" implies that our balance point has been exceeded.

Cardiologist Robert S. Eliot asked the following question of himself when he had a heart attack apparently related to his own profound over-working behavior:

"IS IT WORTH DYING FOR?"

Some of us verbally answer "No" but then through our actions say "Yes." We would rather be dead than feel valueless, and we haven't discovered ways of feeling sufficiently valued except through our excessive working.

Sexual promiscuity is a way of seeking nurture and acceptance.

‹›══◉══‹›

If we believe being "macho" is important to our self image, and being "macho" means "sleeping around," we may "sleep around" in an effort to bolster our low self image. Or if from an early age we received the most affirmation or at least the most attention from parents and others for being "cute" or later for our "grown-up" and "sexy" appearance, then we may become excessively flirtatious when we are older out of a desire for affirmation. If a parent was sexually seductive toward us or involved us in explicitly sexual behavior, then hoping to gain control over the chaos, we may repeat these confusing and frightening scenes over and over again with a variety of partners. While we only want to feel loved, we inadvertently set ourselves up through our casual sexual encounters for more confusion and sorrow as well as shame and guilt.

By its nature, sexual behavior also causes us to be physically close to another person. Sexual gratification is inherently pleasurable and only becomes a source of displeasure when there have been earlier, fear-inducing associations. As a result of a desire for closeness or sexual pleasure, we may seek or agree to sexual experiences which are harmful or at least not helpful to us.

Saying "No" to sex when it is not in the context of an otherwise loving relationship is a way of preserving the specialness of sex. It also avoids the tendency for an otherwise promising relationship to be destroyed or prematurely burdened by emotions and expectations for which the relationship is not yet ready.

We frequently attempt to control the behavior and attitudes of others out of fear.

We may fear others will control us if we don't control them.

We may fear they will withdraw their nurture or acceptance from us unless we control them through maintaining their dependence on us.

We may fear losing some other real or perceived necessity of life which they have helped provide us.

Prejudice and blind hate come from fear.

Fear that our needs will not be met is usually the cause for our angry, belligerent, and aggressive attitudes and behaviors towards others. If we fear that we will lose our job or status to someone else, that person becomes a threat to us. We subsequently feel threatened by all others who we associate with that person in some way.

If we feel others are dominant over us, it is our tendency to resent their dominance and to fear they will deprive us of something we value if they haven't already. If we cannot strike back directly, we are likely to encourage among our friends and others of similar persuasion an undercurrent of hostility towards those who we feel have harmed us or who threaten us.

We might also pick out others who we perceive as weaker than we and attempt our own dominance of them out of our frustration over feeling dominated.

In either case, the resulting atmosphere of hostility makes it likely that a vicious cycle of reciprocal fear and aggression will result. The only hope for deliverance from this vicious cycle is for us to accept the intrinsic value of us all, to see the fear for what it is, and to respond with love, kindness, cooperation and understanding rather than with more fear and aggression.

*Fear of rejection or
other danger to our own well-being
motivates hurtful, self-centered, or
excessively self-sacrificial
behavior and attitudes.*

Abandonment is the ultimate rejection.

Any of us who have been adopted have probably struggled with feelings that our birth parents didn't want us. No matter how loving our adopted parents have been toward us, we have probably had to come to grips with having been put up for adoption in the first place.

If our parents divorced, we may have felt that we were left (abandoned) too. Further, if after divorce, one of our parents gave up the parenting role and hardly ever saw us after that, we have probably had to struggle with our feelings of having been unloved and rejected by that parent.

If a parent or someone close to us commits suicide, then we may experience similar feelings of abandonment and rejection. This is often true even when the death of a parent is from an accident or illness.

We may also feel abandoned and rejected when our parents (or our adult partner for that matter) have been too busy or otherwise too preoccupied to have spent time with us or listened to us. We may begin to feel that we must not matter very much to them.

These feelings of abandonment and rejection can induce further feelings of anxiety or even panic if we don't have sufficient alternative sources for life's necessities (food, clothing, shelter, safety, nurture and acceptance). As small children we are totally dependent on older caregivers, and abandonment would literally mean death if no one came to our rescue.

Trust comes from a combination of good experiences and faith in their continuation.

If we are treated with loving kindness and respect by someone with particular characteristics, then our tendency is to trust this same person, or others with similar personal characteristics, to treat us with similar kindness and respect in the future.

On the other hand, if we are irritably discounted and treated with disrespect and meanness by someone with particular characteristics, then our tendency is to distrust this person, or others with similar personal characteristics, and expect them to act unlovingly toward us in the future. We are likely to try to protect ourselves from further hurt by employing a number of defensive maneuvers, which in some way allow us to avoid this person or diminish our vulnerability when in contact with him or her.

If we have been hurt by a man with a mustache, then we may be wary of all men who wear a mustache. If we have been hurt by someone who speaks softly and smiles a lot, then we may distrust others who have these characteristics, even though soft speech and smiling generally denote safety rather than danger. If we are repeatedly hurt by someone who appears outwardly by most usual signs to be trustworthy, then we will come to distrust these usual signs of safety. This situation may cause us much confusion and may ultimately lead to our not trusting anyone for fear that we have read the signs incorrectly — that rather than a safe situation, we are dealing with someone who will eventually hurt us.

Excessively distrusting attitudes
can be changed,
but only by new experiences
which consistently, over time,
let us know that we do not
have to generalize our earlier,
hurtful experiences
to every remotely similar situation.
We can learn to discriminate
the subtle differences between
dangerous situations and safe ones.

Self-confidence is trusting ourself – trusting our inner resources. The higher our self-confidence, the more we trust our ability to seek and ultimately find solutions to the most complex problems.

Holidays are often painful or at least disappointing.

Holidays are usually associated with getting together with family or, at least, with friends and often cause us to long for times remembered, which are no more, or for times wished for, which have not been and possibly cannot be. In other words, our fantasies about an ideal holiday experience can cause us much pain and disappointment when the reality doesn't live up to our fantasy.

Rather than feeling deprived when we cannot have our ideal holiday experience, it is often helpful to look for satisfying alternatives that are within the realm of possibility.

There are multiple loses associated with divorce.

No matter whether we left, have been left, or mutually agreed to separate, divorce means inevitable feelings of loss which may result in sadness, anger, and depression.

Whatever the circumstances, we may feel like a failure – that we are incompetent when it comes to relationships. This is especially likely if divorce has never or only rarely occurred within our families. We tend to ask ourselves, "Where did I go wrong?" This feeling of being incompetent then tends to pervade all the ways we think and feel about ourselves.

Another loss may be friends who associated with us when we were married but now don't include us in their plans. Our standard of living may be lowered, and our position within our communities may significantly change. In addition, where there are children, they tend to act out their frustrations, thus increasing our feelings of loss of control over our lives.

We may also miss the continuation of a shared history we had experienced with our former partner. Holidays and other special occasions may suddenly feel empty or as though something important is missing. This can be true even when there had been serious and prolonged conflict between us during our marriage to one another. While a part of us may be shouting "good riddance," another part of us is clinging to the shared memories and the unfulfilled hopes and dreams.

There are times when marriages need to be terminated through divorce in order to allow for new beginnings. This is especially true when, after long and diligent effort, neither partner can see any room for reacting differently toward one another, and current behavior is causing us serious physical or emotional harm.

In short, staying together and working out the conflicts is usually desirable. When this is not possible, divorce, even with its inherent losses, may become necessary. And if so, *forgiveness of ourselves and of our former partner is an essential element of a loving, healing attitude.*

*Losing
someone we love
may cause us
to feel
more than sad.*

While we may experience grief primarily as sadness when someone we love dies, we may also experience anger, guilt, depression, and anxiety. We may even believe we see and hear the person with whom we have been so close after their death. All of these feelings can be very confusing and perhaps frightening, especially if we have begun wondering about our own sanity because we fear our thoughts and feelings aren't "normal."

At a time like this, is anger normal? Yes, ANGER very frequently is a part of grief. The angry feelings may be related to our feelings of abandonment, feelings that the death was senseless or unfair, or feelings that our relationship had in some way not been what we had hoped or that there was still unfinished business between us. In any event, there were aspects of the death which were out of our control. Being out of control naturally causes us to feel angry, unless we are secure enough in our beliefs about ourselves and our place in the order of things to accept what we cannot control.

GUILT may be a part of our grief if we believe we could have somehow changed the outcome for the better, if we harbored resentments which never got worked out, or if we have feelings of anger and don't believe we should.

DEPRESSION implies feelings of hopelessness and helplessness which may come from being unable to imagine surviving such a loss — unable to imagine life being worth living without the presence of the one we have lost. Depression may also come from having anger toward the person who has died and being unable to let ourselves admit it or express it.

ANXIETY is sometimes associated with grief when we have depended so much on this person that we are afraid we can't obtain the necessities of life (food, clothing, shelter, safety, nurture, and acceptance) by our own efforts or through others .

All of these feelings may occur together or in rapid succession.

THEY ARE ALL "NORMAL!" Accepting them within ourselves is an important step toward letting go and living within the present while still retaining the important memories we have from the past.

As parents we abuse our children because of feelings of profound frustration over feeling out of control of our own supplies of life's necessities.

Complex memories of deprivation of one kind or another may fuel the fires of frustration which may then reach a flash point in the present.

Our vulnerable children may inadvertently (or even purposely as children will inevitably do from time to time) add to our frustration over feeling out of control. We who have reached a flash point and haven't learned more effective coping strategies may then direct our frustrations toward our children in the form of abuse of one kind or another.

No matter what the circumstances may be, however, it is always our responsibility as parents to avoid abusive behavior. When we are feeling frustrated, we must avoid hurtful actions toward our children and seek alternative, helpful ways of dealing with our fears and feelings of inadequacy. If we cannot find alternative approaches on our own, we must seek the help of a trusted friend or counselor. We must not cover up our negative behavior through denial, for this compounds prior abuse and tends to perpetuate future abusive behavior.

If we are abusive parents, we were often victims of abuse ourselves; and our abused children often will remain victims all of their lives, become abusive themselves, or both.

We tend to repeat in our current life the painful past experiences of our own and of our parents' lives.

Usually without being aware of it, we all tend to set ourselves up to repeat in some way the traumatic events that either we experienced directly as children or experienced indirectly through the distress of a parent — distress we could not adequately comfort or fully understand. We set ourselves up in the present to re-experience our earlier distress out of a usually unconscious desire to achieve mastery over these distressing situations. In other words, we felt out of control and overwhelmed and now somehow repeat the traumatic event with the unconscious hope that this time it will be different. Unfortunately, we usually don't get it quite right or can't believe it when we do and, therefore, continue to repeat the same distressing pattern over and over again.

Another potential unconscious motive for our compulsion to repeat these kinds of patterns is again an attempt at attaining mastery but with a different twist — we identify with an abusive parent or other aggressor, unconsciously believing that by acting now as they did then, we will gain the power they had over us back when we were feeling powerless. Again, the main problem with this kind of solution is that it doesn't work, and our feelings of being powerless are compounded by feelings of guilt for being almost "just like they were."

Jealousy and envy are manifestations of fear.

We have all had feelings of jealousy and will have those feelings again. In every case, at the very least, this jealousy will cause emotional distress for ourselves and others. Among other responses, this distress may be experienced as a gut-wrenching anxiety, tension headaches, explosive angry outbursts, or tearful feelings of rejection. Acting on these feelings in one way or another causes further distress.

Envy is a close relative of jealousy and has similar negative consequences. In addition, it tends to drive us to obtain things and status we do not need and treat others and ourselves in unloving ways in our quest to obtain these things or positions of status.

Both jealousy and envy are manifestations of fear—fear that there won't be enough of life's necessities to go around, and we'll be left out—fear that we will not be able to meet society's misplaced expectations which we have accepted as necessary for our success.

The only way to diminish these emotions and their likely negative consequences is to come to know that we are intrinsically valuable whether or not we are being affirmed by a particular person or persons, and our success is dependent only upon having a loving attitude toward ourselves and others as we go about competently meeting our basic needs.

In our youth-oriented, death-denying culture, aging is often frightening and lonely.

In modern-day societies of the industrially developed countries, if we do not have a firm sense of our personal and corporate value, we may become cynical and bitter as we grow beyond middle age. There is little that is positive popularly associated with aging in our world today. All the TV commercials and billboards encourage us, in the name of one product or another, to "go for the gusto" since we "only go around once in life." There is the implication that we should abandon our concerns for the consequences of our behavior and seek whatever is youthful, exciting, and personally pleasurable. We are not encouraged to consider the effects of our behavior on our tomorrows or those of future generations. If it feels good or makes us appear more sexy, then we are prompted to "go for it." As a result, we often break old commitments, seek younger friends, and try to look and act younger than average for our age. We often try to fool not only everyone else but ourselves as well. Unfortunately perhaps, we cannot change the reality of the aging process, and our efforts to be young usually end in fear and bitterness. We may have cut ourselves off from those who would be most affirming of us and, therefore, spend our advancing years increasingly isolated and lonely.

If only we could understand as a society that beyond meeting our basic needs, freely given service to others in a spirit of love toward ourselves and others is what brings us personal peace and satisfaction. We could then give up searching for the fountain of youth. We could truly enjoy one day at a time no matter what our circumstances, confident that our best efforts for good today will be both rewarding in the present and bear good fruit in someone's future.

For most of us,
the prospect of death
is the ultimate loss of control
and is very frightening.

Our fear probably results from a variety of causes, yet for many of us the principal factor, in addition to the natural biological tendency for self-preservation, is the anticipation of being separated from others who accept and affirm us.

The prospect of death is less frightening for us if we feel we have been affirmed by, and have made a valuable contribution to, the society from which we will be departing. It is also made less frightening if we believe in and anticipate having our spirits accepted into the loving presence of an accepting, forgiving God where we will be preserved in safety for eternity.

When someone we know who is near our own age dies or faces death, we are reminded of our own mortality.

◄►━━◉━━◄►

This can be a very valuable reminder if it causes us to reflect on the way we have been living and, consequently, make adjustments which will result in our being more loving toward ourselves and each other while we live "one day at a time."

We can gain this same perspective, perhaps with even more certainty, if we face death ourselves and then find we have longer to live.

If either the near-death experience or the death of a friend or our own near-death experience causes us to worry fearfully about how much time we have left, we are likely to get ourselves and others into trouble by foolishly indulging ourselves with all kinds of activities which are either directly harmful or indirectly diminish our capacity to be of real service to ourselves or others.

*When we are feeling
utterly overwhelmed
by our emotions or life situation,
we sometimes contemplate suicide.*

If we have felt an extreme paucity of affirmation or acceptance, we may believe death, or even death by suicide, will provide an escape from feelings of degradation and humiliation or will provide a means through self-sacrifice of obtaining some sense of value.

Suicide or suicidal gestures may allow those of us who feel powerless, degraded, and unaffirmed to exercise a measure of control in our lives which we otherwise have not felt we had.

There are <u>always</u>, however, other options short of suicide which can give us a greater sense of control and even allow for affirmation not previously possible. These options, of course, do not seem available to us if we are seriously contemplating suicide.

Thoughts and feelings
may lead to actions,
yet they are not the same as actions.

It may be helpful to reward ourselves
with something pleasurable and
unharmful when we have been able to
avoid acting on thoughts or feelings
which would have had harmful effects if
we had acted upon them.

We are all inherently
problem-solving creatures
and derive special satisfaction
from finding solutions
to even the smallest problems.

In fact, we easily become bored and feel less than useful if we have no problems for which to seek solutions. We like problems; we just don't like to feel overwhelmed by them. When our best efforts to attain mastery over a particular problem don't produce a solution (mastery), we are likely to feel a sense of failure. This will be especially likely if we have been led to believe we should be able to find a solution.

If the problem at hand is achieving a sense of parental or community acceptance, then we are likely to work very hard at trying to meet the standards of acceptability which prevail for our parents or in our community.

If a parent is emotionally or physically distressed, a child is likely to want desperately to solve the problems causing the parent's distress — to heal the parent. Here again this may be attempted through trying to please the parent by meeting or attempting to meet the parent's spoken and unspoken expectations. If the parent is not healed, then the child is likely to feel profound frustration which can lead to anger, depression, trying harder, or giving up.

Will there ever be an end to problems?

The answer is NO, not until we die. And even then problems go on.

Again, we are problem-solving creatures. Like a bulldozer which requires dirt or the like to push around in order to be needed, we must have problems to solve.

Problems are not, therefore, a problem in and of themselves. They only become a problem when we have more problems to solve than we have the means with which to solve them. In that case, we must deal with "too many problems" by setting priorities and working on the most important problems one aspect at a time until each one in turn is solved. The problems which are not realistically solvable by us at this time have to be broken down into even smaller, solvable parts, or we have to accept our inability to solve these problems (or their parts) at this time.

Bad things happen to everybody.

Events in our lives are not always fair.
Bad luck comes to everybody from time
to time, and there is absolutely no reason
for it. We just happen to be in the wrong
place at the wrong time.

When this is our experience, we have
two basic choices after we have
bemoaned our predicament or our loss.
We can stay stuck crying "why me?", or
we can accept what we cannot change,
appreciate the opportunities still
available to us, and move on to the next
phase of our lives.

This is not meant to suggest that we
shouldn't mourn our losses, it is simply
meant to affirm that we always have
choices after the mourning is complete.

Adverse circumstances may sometimes be necessary for positive change to occur.

Often we are unwilling to confront our unhelpful or harmful behaviors and attitudes until we are faced with a crisis of some kind in our own life.

It is, therefore, useful to look for the opportunities for growth which a crisis can afford.

To live joyfully
we have to accept those things
we cannot change,
and
we don't have to like them.

Acceptance of those things we cannot change does not mean apathy! We can always look for loving ways — helpful, unharmful ways — to change unloving circumstances wherever we find them. We may need the help of others, or we may need to wait until a more favorable time when other events have occurred which can make positive change possible.

Acceptance of those things we cannot change does not mean denying our grief and avoiding mourning. We cannot undo tragic, irreversible events, yet it is not helpful to deny our feelings about the loss or tragedy. Feelings have to be worked through, not denied.

We can tolerate our longings.

If we are not facing a threat to our life, our longings are not a cause for panic. We can tolerate more pain than we often think we can.

When we feel hunger, loneliness, sadness, anger, or fear, we do not have to panic. Just because we feel needy, does not mean we have to try frantically to satisfy those feelings of need or deny we feel what we do.

Bad feelings often pass spontaneously. When they don't, we can recover a sense of well-being by recognizing our competence at providing for our basic needs and by putting into action the principles we have learned for living lovingly toward ourselves and others.

Anything worthwhile is worth working and waiting for. While some worthwhile things are free or ought to be (like a smile or an encouraging word for anyone we meet or a hug from a loved one), most worthwhile things require work and waiting.

When we are feeling pessimistic and generally downtrodden, there can be value in focusing on our strengths and on what is going well in spite of the difficulties.

It may also be helpful to consider how this difficult time can be turned into an opportunity for greater understanding of ourselves or others—to consider how it can be an opportunity for a new beginning. There are even times when a difficult situation can be thought of as an adventure which, with patience and positive anticipation, will have an acceptable outcome.

When the details of our lives
seem just too much to bear,
then let us consider
the following strategies
for obtaining relief:

Take time out
Rest
Pray
Meditate
Exercise
Break problems into manageable parts
Prioritize
Talk to ourselves
Share frustrations with others
Seek professional help

Singing can lift our spirits.

While listening to music can be calming and uplifting, our own singing may have even more potential for changing our mood. Selected folk songs, inspirational hymns, broadway musicals, and other popular songs which have an upbeat quality can do much to dispel the blues and put us into a lighter frame of mind.

Singing the blues, however, is not without real value. Sometimes we can release pent-up worries through sad songs which express our pain. Once our feelings are revealed more fully to us through the music, we can get beyond anger to the real work of mourning. Once mourning is completed, there can again be room for joyful tunes and moods.

Singing or playing music with others can help us come closer together and often plays a valuable part in building a more emotionally harmonious community.

We might feel overwhelmed
because sometimes our time
won't stretch far enough
for all we have set for ourselves to do.

◆=◉=◆

When this is true, there are helpful strategies for us to use.

FIRST

We can try, if possible, to become more efficient (organize better and prioritize).

SECOND

If more efficiency is not possible, we can DELEGATE some of what we have to do (if others are willing at the compensation we offer).

If no one can be found to help us for the price we are offering, we can raise the price, if we can afford it and if having help is worth to us paying a higher price.

THIRD

If delegation is not an option for whatever reasons, WE MUST SAY "NO" to some of what we are asking ourselves to do. Saying "NO" may mean, of course, saying "NO" only for a while. More time may become available to us at some point in the future.

We need to be honest with ourselves first, and also with others, about just how much time we have.

*While efficiency and speed
may be very desirable,
HURRY can be deadly
both to our physical well-being
and to our spiritual well-being.*

Hurry causes us to lose patience with ourselves
and others, leading to frustration and loss of
self-esteem for all involved. Seldom does the
end justify being hurried. A more relaxed
alternative can nearly always be found.

*The only solution
to the frantic pursuit of anything
is to come to accept our intrinsic value
and our ability to meet our basic needs
through a balanced implementation of
our own particular talents.*

It is important to do today's work today if at all possible, but it is very important to be realistic about what we expect ourselves to do in a single day. It is also important when making plans for a given week to keep a balance between work, recreation, and the nurturing of relationships. Recreation may include meditation, prayer, exercise, relaxed meal times, rest, contemplation, and play. Work includes making a living, participating in community projects, and learning new skills. The nurturing of relationships includes listening to our friends and loved ones, sharing their joys and pains, and helping each other with our projects.

Sometimes our energy
won't stretch far enough
for all we have set for ourselves to do.

FIRST
We may need to get more sleep. We'll do better work and enjoy our play more when we are rested.

SECOND
Meditation may help us relax and focus our energies rather than waste energy spinning our wheels.

THIRD
Changing our eating habits may provide us with more energy. Heavy meals can cause us to be sluggish, and inadequate diets can leave us weak and without stamina.

FOURTH
Aerobic exercise is profoundly energizing and can increase significantly our efficiency.

FIFTH
Resolution of emotional conflicts will also free energy for other activities.

Sometimes our money won't stretch far enough for all we have set for ourselves to do.

When this is true, we have to ask ourselves some hard questions about our priorities.

FIRST
We have to be honest with ourselves about how much money we really have to spend and what are our real fixed expenses (for real necessities).

SECOND
Once we know just how much money we have to spend after accounting for anticipated, fixed (necessary) expenses, it will be most helpful to ask ourselves:

Do I or my community really need this particular purchase? Do I or my community really want this particular purchase given the other needs and wants we have and the resources we have available?

THIRD
It is helpful to think not only of ourselves and our more immediate communities (families and near neighbors) but also of our more distant communities (state, nation, world). In addition to cash resources, natural and human resources need to be budgeted in this same fashion.

When unexpected circumstances
demand more time, energy,
money, or other resources
than planned or available,
it is most helpful to be
as _flexible_ as possible.

Organizing
according to <u>priority</u>
those aspects of our lives
which <u>can be</u> controlled
will allow for
a greater sense of mastery
and peace.

⟨⟩══◉══⟨⟩

At the end of a day there will inevitably be things left undone, but the most important things will have been accomplished, or progress will have been made toward their accomplishment.

If we have a large task or series of tasks to perform, it is helpful to break the whole into manageable parts, and do one part each and every day until the whole project is completed. If we miss a day, it is important to get back on schedule the next day without trying to make up for the missed portion.

Peace implies
an acceptance of
personal and community limits.

✦═◉═✦

None of us can have or do
everything at once.

✦═◉═✦

Choices always preclude
other choices.

Seldom does anything have to be
all or nothing.
The best available approximation
of a balance between the extremes
is usually desirable.

We will never achieve our ideals,
though it is helpful
to strive toward them.
We will be happiest if we appreciate
what we are and have
rather than being
chronically dissatisfied
with what we are not or do not have.

*Remember, when we are feeling intense emotions,
it is helpful to ask ourselves,*

"Is my life really in immediate danger?"

When faced with a real or perceived threat to our supplies of life's necessities (food, clothing, shelter, safety, nurture, and acceptance), we can: 1) panic or despair, 2) become angry, or 3) have hope that we can discover other options for getting our needs met.

"Am I in danger of starving, could I die from exposure, am I in immediate danger of being killed or raped?" If the answer is yes, then we must protect ourselves in the best ways we can think of. If the answer is no, then we can relax some and ask, "am I afraid of rejection, abandonment, losing my identity, losing my independence, of not being valued, or of being out of control?" If we answer yes to any of these questions, then is our fear coming from the current situation we are facing, or is it left over from an earlier time in our lives?

Knowing where our fear is coming from helps us know where to look for solutions. Reacting to our fear without asking these questions is like shooting in the dark and makes hitting the target almost impossible, thus increasing our sense of failure and frustration.

It is important to talk to ourselves in affirming, loving ways.

We need to remind ourselves of our intrinsic value no matter how beaten down by parents or others we have felt in the past.

We need to remind ourselves of our potential for acting lovingly and avoid the negative self-statements which say we are worthless or otherwise incapable of loving behavior.

We need to avoid "I can't" or "I don't deserve" and instead say:

"I can and will be loving today toward myself and others."

"I was born to be treated lovingly, and so was everyone else."

"If others don't understand about love, I can still try my best to be loving in all the ways which are open to me now!"

"I approve of myself."

"I already have within me the capacity to get what I really need."

"I am whole and complete."

Our minds and our bodies are one! Emotional turmoil and physical illness are inseparable!

We often think of ourselves as somehow split into two parts, mind and body. We tend to think of our emotions as coming from our mind and our physical ailments being a problem with our bodies. Frequently, we even make a further assumption that emotional illness, being "only in our minds," is unreal; and that physical illness, given a known disorder, is real. If we are told that our physical illness is "psychosomatic," we often believe that that means we are not really sick.

These perspectives and assumptions could not be further from the truth! While it may be somewhat useful for conceptualizing some conditions, the mind/body split does not really exist! Problems of metabolism, for instance, may have as much of an effect on our emotions as on our weight or other physical signs or symptoms. Fears left over from a traumatic adult or childhood experience may cause altered blood chemistries as well as crippling emotional distress.

Just because recurrent eye infections in a particular person can be traced to an unresolved psychological conflict, does not make the problem unreal. Antibiotics are still needed for the present bacterial eye infection, while resolution of the psychological conflict is needed before they cease to recur.

Hormonal imbalances of all kinds cause a combination of physical and emotional problems. Medications given for a physical problem may induce emotional problems, and medications given for emotional problems may induce physical problems. Anxiety can cause high blood pressure and other physical problems, while all sorts of physical problems can cause anxiety. Alcohol abuse can cause both emotional and physical problems, while craving for alcohol is probably, at least in some of us, genetically inherited. We might want a divorce from our spouse because we're depressed due to a vitamin deficiency, or we might be depressed and have an ulcer because our marriage is in trouble. The list could go on and on. Dividing our problems into purely "medical," "psychological," or "psychiatric" is always a big mistake!

Psychotherapy
can be helpful
at times when we have trouble
affirming that we are lovable or
if we need better problem-solving skills.
Some healing aspects of
psychotherapy include:

– the opportunity to share our distress honestly with another person who cares about us and wishes to know in as complete a way as possible what our pain has been like.

– the opportunity to have a person with a more objective perspective (due to not being immersed in our particular situations) share his or her ideas for helpful, alternative coping strategies.

– the opportunity within a safe setting to look at earlier feelings of hurt, fear, and guilt which may be contributing to our current distress.

– the opportunity to discover the repetitive patterns in our life which are harmful or unhelpful and which have their origins in our earlier traumatic experiences. Conscious awareness of these patterns allows us more latitude in our options for present and future behavior.

Medications can sometimes be very helpful in treating illness ("emotional" or "physical") when the illness is caused by or made worse by a physiological imbalance of some kind which can be corrected or improved by a particular medicine or combination of medicines.

Psychological imbalances may sometimes result from taking medicines to correct a physiological problem; i.e., medicine for high blood pressure can sometimes cause depression in certain individuals. Physiological imbalances may also result from insufficient exercise and rest, from dietary excesses or insufficiencies, from exposure to harsh natural or manufactured elements (like various kinds of environmental pollutions), from hormonal changes which occur for various reasons, and from insufficient nurture and acceptance.

While it is very important to correct any correctable detrimental influences, medicines may be very helpful (even lifesaving) temporary or perhaps long-term aids in attempting to re-establish physiological balance.

Secrets always need to be shared.

Secrets of any kind, especially family secrets which we have been admonished not to tell under threat of dire consequences, definitely need to be shared with at least one other trusted person. Otherwise, we tend to develop feelings of guilt, fear, depression, and anxiety which can seriously affect our capacity to be loving toward ourselves and others.

The fears of humiliation associated with having a personal or family secret known always loom larger for us than the reality of having it known would warrant. If we believe having our secret known would lead to our prosecution under the law or other harm to ourselves or to someone else, however, then we may need to share it in confidence with someone whose judgment we trust.

No secret about which we feel shame should ever be carried alone, for the burden always becomes larger over the years and affects our life decisions in adverse ways. Whatever may be the reality of the initial behavior or circumstances which we have kept secret, they are compounded in direct or indirect ways through the secret.

Sharing a secret is not the same as betraying a confidence. A secret carries a personal burden of shame and guilt, while a confidence is something we know about, but about which we carry no personal shame or guilt. It is important to maintain a confidence (unless doing so would cause imminent harm), while it is important to share our personal secrets with at least one other person.

The truth shall set us free!

Sharing the truth about those parts of ourselves of which we have been ashamed or felt guilty does, indeed, set us free to live more positively in the present.

Can we ever really redress the ways we have been hurtful to ourselves and to others?

No, we cannot, not if we mean <u>completely</u> making right what we have done wrong. We cannot completely undo the effects of our unhelpful and hurtful behavior and replace it with the effects loving behavior would have rendered under the same circumstances.

Loving behavior could have had unseen, positive ramifications which could have been extended far beyond the setting in which we were acting. Similarly, our unloving behavior may have had unseen, negative ramifications far beyond the setting in which we were acting. Since we cannot go back in time, it is, therefore, impossible to completely redress the ways we have been hurtful to ourselves and others.

On the other hand, we may be able to significantly improve the situation as it now stands. Through an apology or some other attempt at making peace, we may help change some of the negative effects of our previous, unloving behavior towards others. There are times, of course, when saying or doing anything else would cause more harm than good. In these instances it is probably best to "leave well enough alone," and just try to learn from our mistakes.

It is always important to apologize to ourselves for the hurtful things we have done to ourselves, and resolve to change the way we treat ourselves in the present and future. We may be able to only partially undo the damage we have done to ourselves, but we can probably prevent or diminish further damage. When is the time to make these changes? As soon as possible!!

Worry not about anything about which we can do nothing.

It is helpful to adopt an attitude which precludes worrying about anything which is out of our control.

For that matter, it is also helpful to avoid worrying about anything we can control.

It is important to make prudent plans for the future, but it is not helpful to worry today about how something will turn out tomorrow.

Worry is simply not helpful. We benefit most from letting go of worry and doing what we can. If we put the same energy into taking whatever small steps toward our goals that are available to us as we would have spent worrying, we might be surprised how quickly many of our problems disappear.

A community spirit of love —
of mutual respect and cooperation —
can change our worries
to accomplishments.

That which seems either impossible or terribly burdensome when confronted by an individual can be accomplished, and perhaps even joyfully so, when undertaken by a loving community.

If we enlist someone else to voluntarily help us, and their assistance is appreciated, then any task, no matter how tough, can be satisfying for all involved.

Everyday can be
an adventure if we are receptive
to the opportunities
for enrichment and growth
which come our way.

If we can accept what could not be and cannot be, then we can be free to experience what <u>can</u> be. We have to let go of many old rituals and prejudices in the process, but we can gain far more than we release. We can only let go of the old rituals and prejudices, however, after coming to trust that every present day can bring us new opportunities for enrichment and growth.

When faced with adversity and pain, we can find opportunities to give and receive love — sometimes in the most unexpected places.

Seemingly everyday occurences can even be experienced in a new, adventurous perspective.

Living as fully as possible in each present day is a helpful goal. An awareness of the future (potential consequences of present actions) and of the past (positive memories and useful lessons) is important, but it is best that this awareness be secondary to enjoying today.

A journal of our adventures and other good experiences can be helpful to us during times of stress.

If each day in a journal we note any adventures or other positive experiences we've had, we can later turn to our notes to help us recall these positive feelings when faced with periods of increased stress and anxiety. We can then remember how we were surprised by our good problem-solving ability in a certain situation or how much we have enjoyed someone important in our lives who is now causing us irritation or other distress.

A photo album of our good experiences can also be used in a similar way.

All of us can be competent within the framework of our own unique abilities.

COMPETENCE is having sufficient ability to deal adequately with the day-to-day aspects of our lives. It implies being good enough. We do not have to be the best in order to be competent.

Competence is not dependent upon being better than someone else, and it cannot be attained through putting down others.

If we have developed a sense of competence through being able to cope with burdensome situations, then there may be a tendency to always carry a burden or carry a burden longer than necessary in order to maintain the sense of competence attained through being a masterful carrier of burdens. We need to be aware of this possibility so we may be more likely to avoid this behavior when it becomes unloving toward ourselves or others.

*Being honest with ourselves
about what we cannot
personally control and
coming to accept that our competence
is not dependent upon
controlling everything
can contribute toward peace
(personal and otherwise).*

Our competence does not depend upon having it recognized by everyone else.

While we all need affirmation of our acceptance by others, we will not have enough in common with all others for everyone to be affirming of everything we do or say. Abraham Lincoln is reputed to have said something like, "We can please all the people some of the time, some of the people all of the time, but not all the people all the time." This maxim is true for all of us all of the time.

We often, however, act and react as though we should be able to please everyone under all circumstances. This seems to be especially true of those of us who have not felt "good enough" to please an overly demanding parent or heal a chronically ill or impaired parent. In search of feeling "good enough", we may have become praise junkies. We attempt to boost our flagging spirits by working very hard to secure praise from everyone. When we are unsuccessful in this effort, we tend to feel deflated, dejected, and unloved, even if nearly everyone is telling us how much they appreciate us.

An approach to finding a solution to this kind of problem is to frequently say affirming statements to ourselves while remembering that OUR COMPETENCE DOES NOT DEPEND UPON HAVING IT RECOGNIZED BY EVERYONE ELSE.

When one of us in
an unbalanced community
begins to shift toward
a more balanced position,
the community (from family
to increasingly larger communities)
may strongly resist the change
and bring great pressure to bear on us
to maintain the status quo.

If we find ourselves in an unbalanced community which is having a harmful influence on our own ability to achieve and maintain a relatively balanced, loving attitude, it is important to attempt to respond to this community in a way which will preserve our balance and encourage or permit greater balance within the community. When our best efforts over a prolonged period of time have not made it possible for us to attain and maintain relative balance within this community, it may be helpful to withdraw from this community at least temporarily, if not permanently. At times like these, it is very important to find another more loving community within which we are warmly welcome. This may not be possible, yet it is certainly worth seeking.

Some of our parenting needs can be met through adult friends other than our parents.

We all have needs for nurture and acceptance which our parents may not be able to meet due to a variety of factors. These may include our parents' emotional or physical impairments, their misunderstanding of our needs, our inability to convey our needs to them, or external circumstances beyond their control or ours. Whatever the reasons, there have been, and will be again, times when we have needed more parenting than our parents were able to give us.

Since our needs for nurture and acceptance can be truly needs and not just wants, it is helpful to develop alternative sources from which to receive them.

It is not helpful to try to get these needs met through our own young children, but we can establish a network of friends through whom we may receive what we need and give what they need. These friends may be younger or older than we. The only requirement is that we be able to mutually share of ourselves in a spirit of love.

Competence generally implies
being able to abide by the rules
or laws of our community.
Rules or laws and the consequences
for breaking them are established
in order to help prevent
hurtful behavior and foster
helpful behavior. In other words,
good rules or good laws
promote relative peace and tranquility
for both individuals and communities.

Following every usually helpful rule to the letter all of the time may
not, however, be possible or even desirable; yet it is important to be
honest with ourselves about the likely consequences of breaking the
rule and be prepared to accept the consequences if we do.

*When there are no rules or
questionable rules
to cover a particular situation,
it is important to ask ourselves
if the behavior under consideration
will be helpful to us and to others
and will it contribute toward
a good (loving) outcome?*

*A good end cannot justify
unloving means,
, nor must we ever be unloving
that good may come of it.
Let us then try what love will do;
for if another did once see
we love them, we should soon find
they would not harm us.*

Adapted from a quote by William Penn 1693

Penn's second sentence does not apply when we are a relatively powerless child experiencing abuse from a disturbed, more powerful adult. This distinction is critical, for no amount of loving behavior by the child can prevent the abusive behavior of the distrubed, fearful adult.

*We benefit
from listening to our intuitions,
yet before acting on them
we need to measure them
against what we know
to be loving and good.*

Holding a grudge or seeking revenge consumes otherwise useful time and energy and tends to rob us of our creativity.

◆◇══◉══◇◆

Forgiving others for their behavior which has been harmful in some way to us is in our best interest. Through forgiveness we become free to live joyfully in the present rather than remaining shackled to the hurts and fears of our past.

It is impossible to move from resentment to forgiveness as long as we still feel threatened. Often there is an unconscious fear associated with a past experience which we felt powerless to prevent. Getting in touch with our old feelings of helplessness and taking steps to feel mastery over similar situations in the present can free us from fear and allow us to forgive rather than resent.

People who have wronged us have done so because of their own fears or illness. They are more likely to be influenced to change their harmful ways through our love and concern rather than through our hate or indifference. Even if their change is impossible no matter what we do or do not do, we will benefit from avoiding the negative effects our hate has on us.

We do, however, need to remember the harmful experiences so that we can protect ourselves and others from similar hurt in the present or future. If there have been no appreciable changes in those people or situations which have hurt us in the past, then we don't benefit anyone by letting the hurtful experiences be repeated. Protecting ourselves is not the same as holding a grudge or seeking revenge.

When our personal safety is being seriously threatened, is there a place for a violent response?

Yes, as an absolutely last resort when all other resources available for self-protection have been exhausted. Under these circumstances, it is justifiable to use sufficient but not excessive force to protect ourselves from sustaining serious injury.

The important qualifying phrases above are "when all other resources available... have been exhausted" and "sufficient but not excessive force." Effective, nonviolent responses are usually available if we look for them and are patient enough to allow them to work. We often react violently because we haven't developed a larger repertoire (range of options) of non-violent responses.

There are times, however, when imminent danger leaves us only the choice of hurting someone or of being seriously injured or killed ourselves. Then the most loving response is to subdue our attacker with "sufficient but not excessive force" to protect us from serious harm. By preventing someone from seriously hurting us, we are not only protecting ourselves, we may also be helping the other person avoid more serious legal or negative interpersonal consequences.

Should we ever use force to protect ourselves from humiliation – to protect our honor? No, we best demonstrate being honorable by trying to find a nonviolent solution to a conflict or, if possible, by walking away from it when another nonviolent solution is not forthcoming. We can be relatively safe without being in total control of what others say or do.

USUALLY VIOLENCE INDUCES MORE VIOLENCE –
ULTIMATELY THERE ARE NO WINNERS,
JUST LOSERS.

*Our loving response is required
for completion of our understanding
of the importance of love and
a loving balance.*

If we have understanding of the value of love
and of maintaining a balanced perspective, yet
do not act in a loving, balanced way toward
ourselves and each other, then we have
nothing. The final, essential ingredient of love
is a loving response to our knowledge of love.

When we know about love and then back up
our knowledge with actions consistent with it,
love is complete!

The more we experience the giving and
receiving of "complete love" – love in action –
the more we truly understand its value.

*Competence is being able
to deal adequately with
the day-to-day aspects of our lives
while putting love into action.
But because we want to feel
in control of as much of our lives
as possible, we long for knowledge of
the "meaning of life"—for a
satisfactory understanding of how,
where, and when we fit into the world.*

We seek an understanding of our relationship to the rest of the universe — a perspective on how we fit into the overall scheme of things.

For those of us who believe in God, God is the Ultimate Organizing Principle — The Ultimate Reality. For those of us who don't believe in an ultimate reality, our sense of how we fit into the overall scheme of things is still important to us and affects how comfortably we are able to deal with the day-to-day aspects of our lives.

If, whatever else God may be,
God is love, truth, and goodness,
then when we embrace
those values of our society
which are not loving, true, or good,
we are separate from God.

God is equally both male and female; poor and rich; weak and strong; old, young, and in between; red, yellow, black, and white. God has no special preference for any particular aspect of God but embraces all of humankind which was made in the image of God. God is not fear, ignorance, jealousy, envy, or resentment but rather love, sharing, cooperation, forgiveness, and enlightenment. God embodies all our highest ideals while loving us with our blemishes and shortcomings.

The spirit of God dwells within us, but we cannot hope to fully understand the will of God. We can only hope to learn, by the grace of God, that God is God and we are not.

Evil is hurtful behavior which results from believing we are more special than someone else.

Evil results from thinking we are more entitled than the next person to the necessities of life. It comes from acting on the belief that our differences justify unkind, disrespectful, cruel, or indifferent behavior toward another.

We cannot isolate ourselves from others based on race, cultural or national origin, sexual preference, gender, or religion without opening the door to evil. Anything which emphasizes our differences rather than acknowledging our similarities and ultimate connectedness and interdependence sets us up for doing harm.

All of creation is one body made of a myriad of precisely balanced interdependent parts. We are separate from each other and need to respect our individual boundaries, but we are also inextricably connected to each other and to all that surrounds us.

We have a right to get our individual needs met and a right to our own ideas and opinions, and so does everyone else. Evil is overcome by finding a balance between meeting our individual needs and our collective needs. Evil is overcome by forgiving ourselves and others for not living up to our ideals.

Evil is overcome by patience and tolerant communication. Evil is overcome by loving our enemies.

However it happened that we are here, we are not here through our own doing.

We are not born through our own efforts nor can we avoid our inevitable death. Our great-great-grand-children are unlikely to remember us a few decades from now, and neither will anyone else for that matter. No matter how famous or infamous we may become, memory of our presence on this earth soon fades. It is important, therefore, that we recognize our humble place in time and live each moment in gratitude to a Power in the universe greater than ourselves for our consciousness of the world around us – for our very existance.

Fame and power are not lasting, and none of us alone can change the world very much for good or ill. We can, however, in concert with others leave it a little better or a little worse than we found it. Let us hope that we of the present group of humans leave it a little better.

The purpose of our lives may be to appreciate creation in all its complexity.

We may have been created for the purpose of appreciating creation.

As far as we know, humans are the only creatures capable of careful inquiry into the nature of the world around us and of reflecting on what we discover.

Everywhere we look there is something wonderful and awe-inspiring. Whether we consider the birth of a new creature, the cycle of the seasons, the beauty of a sunrise, the neurochemistry of a brain, the process of photosynthesis, the rhythm of social inter-actions, or the expansiveness of the heavens, we are struck by how intricate, powerful, and utterly amazing our world truly is.

If we believe in God
(whether we are Jewish,
Christian, Islamic, or Hindu),
how do we love God?

We love God by:
— appreciating and treating respectfully all of God's
Creation including our environment, all creatures
large and small, other people, and ourselves.
— remembering that Goodness is of God, and God's
directions to us help us find and maintain
harmony with the rest of Creation.

Through loving God, we live more abundantly since God's
purposes, as revealed in the scriptures and through God's prophets,
are synonymous with joyful living and harmonious equilibrium or
balance within all of Creation.

*The surrender of our will to God,
a power greater than we, allows us
to accept our place in a harmonious
universe and essentially give up
trying to control those things in our
lives over which we are powerless.*

Our prayer might daily be:

O God, creator and sustainer of the universe, thank you for loving us just as we are whether or not anyone else seems to right now.

Thank you for loving us even though you don't approve of our immature, fear-induced thoughts and behavior.

Please help us feel your strength and security today.

Help us become less fearful and so focused on ourselves.

Allow us to release our need for all things to go the way we think they should.

Help us and all our sisters and brothers of the world seek your guidance which always is available to us if we quietly listen to your still, small voice within.

Please help us to know always in our knowing place that even until our death and beyond death you will keep loving your creation.

Amen.

Do religious rituals cause more good than harm?

Yes, sometimes; perhaps even usually. Religious rituals and other organized religious practices can serve many positive purposes. Rituals can, through the repetition of symbolic acts convey the essence of important concepts, the full significance of which may not be appreciated until some later stage of development on the part of the individual partcipant or even on the part of the corporate participants.

When two or more of us share in religious practices, we can experience a sense of community which can often be affirming, nurturing, and internally balancing. We can convey to one another (especially to our children) knowledge of the helpful, guiding principles which are a part of our traditions. In other words, we can support each other in times of crisis, share our joys, and encourage our best efforts to live lovingly. We can express our gratitude to God for loving us, forgiving us, and guiding us.

So far the case for "more good" in these rituals seems strong. There are, however, potential problems. When rituals perpetually obscure rather than illuminate the spirit behind their inception, they have crossed the line into being harmful! When they become an onerous burden or an opportunity for pretense rather than substance, they have crossed this line as well.

In short, any religious practice which is truly helpful and not hurtful to us does "more good than harm." Any practice which demeans us or causes us all too often "to sweat the small stuff" is likely to do more harm than good. We especially want to guard against rituals becoming the ends in themselves rather than a means toward achieving greater personal and corporate spiritual maturity (which implies loving attitudes and actions) and toward expressing our joyful gratitude to God.

We all have a right to our preferences.

While we do not have a right to behave in ways which will harm others, we do have a right to our own ideas.

Where harm to others or to ourselves is really not in question, our preferences are as valid as anyone's. We do not have to justify them; we have a right to them!

We also have a right to change our minds — to agree with someone with whom we have previously disagreed. And we have a right to maintain our preferences in the face of strenuous opposition — a right to disagree. We may even agree to disagree.

Often our differences are less important than our desire for respect and appreciation.

"Twelve Step" programs: How can they fit into our efforts toward becoming more competent?

Physicians and others (probably all of us know of examples) have witnessed profound emotional and physical cures in people who have had personal, spiritual conversion experiences. People who felt hopelessness in the face of their troubles have found hope and recovery through their faith and trust in a Power greater than themselves. For some of us these changes in our faith and understanding have occurred very quickly, like turning on a light switch, while for others of us the changes have been more gradual.

Those of us who have grown up in churches where we felt exclusiveness and hypocrisy rather than love and acceptance may be reluctant to seek a spiritual solution to our troubles. Those of us who hate ourselves and have not seen our value reflected in the face of another who really knows us may also be reluctant to seek spiritual solutions. Those of us who believe anything not yet scientifically proven is superstitious and silly (if not humiliating evidence of immature gullibility) are not likely to seek spiritual solutions either. On the other hand, when we have hit the bottom emotionally and physically, we may become willing to try anything in order to get out of the terrible place in which we have found ourselves. If we feel incompetent to deal relatively comfortably with the day-to-day aspects of our lives and feel we are not really good enough or that there is no real meaning or purpose in our lives, then we may be willing to seek a spiritual solution in spite of our previous prejudices.

The Twelve-Step programs, of which Alcoholics Anonymous was the first, combine an acknowledgment of our inability thus far to attain balance in our lives (our lives are seriously out of control in one or more ways) and a belief that a Higher Power can help us restore the balance we need and seek. There are specific additional steps which guide our "steps" along the path toward balance and a richer, fuller life.

The Twelve Steps of Twelve-Step Programs

1. We admitted we were powerless over [the unbalanced aspects of our lives] — that our lives had become unmanageable.

2. Came to believe that a Power greater than ourselves could restore us to [balance].

3. Made a decision to turn our will and our lives over to the care of God as we understood [God].

4. Made a searching and fearless moral inventory of ourselves.

5. Admitted to God, to ourselves and to other human beings the exact nature of our wrongs [to others and to ourselves].

6. Were entirely ready to have God remove all these defects of character.

7. Humbly asked [God] to remove our shortcomings.

8. Made a list of all persons [including ourselves] we had harmed, and became willing to make amends to them all.

9. Made direct amends to such people wherever possible, except when to do so would injure them or others.

10. Continued to take personal inventory and when we were wrong promptly admitted it.

11. Sought through prayer and meditation to improve our conscious contact with God as we understood [God], praying only for knowledge of [God's] will for us and the power to carry that out.

12. Having had a spiritual awakening as the result of these steps, we tried to carry this message to others, and to practice these principles in all our affairs.

Adapted from The Twelve Steps of Alcoholics Anonymous World Services, Inc. Copyright ©1939. Please note: the brackets are my way of indicating that I have changed the wording slightly from the original. In the instances above, the wording has been changed to make it more inclusive in some way for all of us no matter what our personal characteristics or the nature of our unbalanced approaches to life.

For Atheists,
God dose not exist.
Values may or may not
take the needs of others
into consideration.

There is no unified perspective which can generally be attributed to those of us who consider ourselves to be atheists other than a belief that there is no ultimate reality (God).

Some of us who are atheists may have high moral values with regard to interpersonal relationships and issues concerning protection of our environment, while others may not.

For some, concern for economic justice may be of prime importance.

For others of us, personal safety from humiliation and abuse may be a focus of our concern.

To be sure, however, all of us whether atheists or believers in God have the same needs for food, clothing, shelter, safety, nurture, and acceptance. All of us are motivated to control our supply of these necessities, and true success in life will inevitably require affirmative expressions of love toward ourselves and each other.

Acting responsibly to protect our environment is an especially important way for us to be loving toward ourselves and others.

Whatever our perspectives about the nature or existence of a Higher Power, it is imperative that we all take whatever steps which are open to us to avoid doing harm, especially irreparable harm, to our environment, which is essential for our continued healthy existence, both individually and collectively.

While nature can compensate and adapt in response to extensive environmental injuries, there are limits to the natural compensatory mechanisms — at least without there being significant, undesirable changes which ultimately could be incompatible with life as we have known it.

The world needs to discover a balanced synthesis of two ideals, one American and the other socialist.

In an ideal world there would be a spirit of cooperation which would encourage all of us as members of the world community to consider the priorities of everyone else in the world as we set our own priorities. The "greatest good for the greatest number" is a principle which is consistent with this spirit as long as the basic needs of all INDIVIDUALS are never forsaken involuntarily for the interests of the majority.

The inalienable individual rights of The First Amendment to The Constitution of The United States of America are considered in the U.S.A. to be "basic needs," while in socialist countries "basic needs" are adequate food, clothing, shelter, and medical care.

Rather than adopt either of these definitions of "basic needs" exclusive of the other, it would be far better to join forces as a world community in which no one person is allowed to have excesses above a certain level until the basics of both The First Amendment AND adequate housing, food, clothing, and medical needs are provided for all inhabitants of the world. In order for this to be possible, while avoiding irresponsible exploitation of our environmental resources, it might be necessary to encourage vigorously the limitation of the world's human population. At least limit the population until technological developments make it possible to provide the comprehensive basic needs to all without doing irreparable harm to the environment which belongs to us all and to all future generations.

How could this synthesis between individual rights and collective rights be attained?

First, we have to come to understand that we are all in this together – that our world has become so small as the result of technological developments, increases in the global human population, and intertwined national economies that we can no longer pretend that we can safely isolate ourselves from each other. We are capable of ruining our entire world environment with all kinds of chemical, biological, and nuclear pollutants even if warfare never becomes a factor.

Second, we must preserve the opportunity for individual economic incentives while not allowing any single individual or small group of individuals (in business corporations or govenments) to exert so much power that they cannot be prevented from doing irreparable harm to the environmental birthright of us all.

Third, we must spread the news that true success does not come from more and more wealth and power but rather from meeting our basic needs and having a loving attitude toward ourselves and equally toward others. This loving attitude must be demonstrated by our respect for ourselves and for the rights of others. After meeting our own basic needs, freely given service to others within our own unique limitations can then replace self-centered and ultimately unsatisfying greed and provide us with genuine mutual satisfaction.

In a more loving world, corporations will still be concerned about profits, but there will be a different "bottom line."

A loving corporate attitude would result in quality products at a fair price with managers and workers sharing in decisions and in profits. Our shared environment would be respected and not sacrificed for short-term profits. At least fifty-one percent of corporate stock would be held by workers, managers, and other community members who have more than invested capital at stake in corporate decisions.

A world community
which has adopted love
as the ultimate definition of success
will reflect our collective maturity and
competence.

*Where there is [love] and wisdom,
there is [less] fear [and] ignorance.*

*Where there is patience and humility,
there is [less] anger [and] vexation.*

*Where there are [modest yet
sufficient circumstances] and joy,
there is [less] greed [and] avarice.*

*Where there is peace and meditation,
there is [less] anxiety [and] doubt.*

Adapted from
FRANCIS OF ASSISI
1181-1226

We can love all humankind,
yet we can truly express that love
only one person at a time.

No matter where we are or with whom, every day we have opportunities to express love. These opportunities are usually fairly simple and include a smile, a friendly greeting, a kind word or deed, an understanding nod, a forgiven slight, a word of encouragement, open-minded attention, and quiet acceptance. At times an opportunity for expressing love may be gentle, but firm limit setting.

Living simply and sharing freely of ourselves and our resources, even in small ways, are also expressions of love.

Being receptive to others and to their expressions of love toward us enriches all involved.

It is helpful to remember how large an impact our small behaviors and utterances can have on our world. One person at a time, one minute at a time, our world can change for the better. We <u>can</u> make a difference.

My best
effort to do good
today
is important
and sufficient!

<u>Best</u> — *my best, not someone else's — also, my best may vary widely dependent upon my emotional or physical state or other circumstances beyond my control to change.*

<u>Good</u> — *contribute toward the corporate good — be loving toward myself and others.*

<u>Today</u> — *we only have today; we cannot undo yesterday or fully anticipate tomorrow.*

<u>Important</u> — *we are a part of a corporate effort, and everyone's contribution large or small is important — the body of humankind is diminished by the loss of any individual contribution.*

<u>Sufficient</u> — *everyone working together can provide all that is needed.*

There is value in

"just" playing.

"just" sitting.

"just" walking.

"just" looking.

"just" dancing.

"just" whistling.

"just" talking.

"just" sunning.

"just" listening.

"just" thinking.

"just" singing.

"just" hugging.

A Few Closing Words From The Author

I have had the good fortune of having some very good teachers along the way. These teachers have been in the form of people and experiences. As a physician, I have had the opportunity to learn many lessons from those who have sought my help. I am very grateful to them for all they have taught me.

I am especially grateful to a Power greater than I which has sustained me and led me when I did not think there was a way out of my troubles. I hope this material reflects this gratitude without any sense of coercion toward others to adopt a particular understanding of a Transcendent Power.

The realities of infantile sexuality and the family romance described by Sigmund Freud and elaborated further by others have not been a subject of this book, but that does not negate their significance in our lives. The psychological theories of many others also have obvious relevance. Many of the ideas contained in those theories are woven into my own thinking and, therefore, into what I have written.

My purpose in writing this material is to share with as many others as I can the ideas and principles which have been helpful to me and to others who have come to me for assistance. Little, if any, of what I have written is new, yet I hope I have said some of it in a way that some can understand and put into practice in a way they have not previously found possible.

The Center for Creative Balance

The Center for Creative Balance is a place where anyone seeking to balance their involvement in the busy world of making a living and raising a family with spiritual, physical, and community fitness is offered education, encouragement, and opportunities for practicing the life skills which lead to balance.

If you would like a catalogue of other materials available from the Center for Creative Balance, please write:

Center for Creative Balance
P.O. Box 16562
Chapel Hill, NC 27514

A small pamphlet which may be of interest is *Peace Pilgrim's Steps Toward Inner Peace* which can be obtained at no charge by writing:

Friends of Peace Pilgrim
43480 Cedar Avenue
Hemet, California 92344
(714) 927-7678

Couples who wish a helpful guide to resolving their differences are encouraged to read *Getting The Love You Want* by Harvel Hendrix.

Another book which is highly recommended is *Who Needs God* by Harold Kushner.